The Morning Smile Collection

Edited by Norris McDonald

Illustrated by Anthony Jenkins

Editorial cartoons by Brian Gable

I(T)P® Nelson

an International Thomson Publishing company

Toronto • Albany • Bonn • Boston • Cincinnati • Detroit • London • Madrid • Melbourne • Mexico City • New York • Pacific Grove • Paris • San Francisco • Singapore • Tokyo • Washington

I(T)P™
International Thomson Publishing
The ITP logo is a trademark under licence

Published in 1997 by
I(T)P Nelson
A division of Thomson Canada Limited
1120 Birchmount Road
Scarborough, Ontario M1K 5G4

Visit our Web site at **http://www.nelson.com/nelson.html**

Canadian Cataloguing in Publication Data

Main entry under title
  The Morning Smile Collection

Collection of "Your Morning Smile" from *The Globe and Mail.*
ISBN 0-17-606821-X

1. Canadian wit and humor (English).
2. Caricatures and cartoons—Canada.
I. McDonald, Norris, 1942–

PS8375.M67   1996   C817'.5408   C96-990099-6
PN6178.C3M67   1996

Printed and bound in Canada

1 2 3 4 (WC) 00 99 98 97

Contents

Preface

You know, when you walk into just about any bookstore in Canada and go over to the humour section, you will likely find something missing: funny Canadian stuff.

Oh, you'll find lots of humour written by the late American housewife Irma Bombeck, and lots of humour written by American newspaper columnist Dave Barry, and lots of Garfield cartoons and Doonesbury collections, and so on, but you won't find much that's really and truly all-Canadian.

Which is why *The Globe and Mail* and ITP Nelson have teamed up to publish *The Morning Smile Collection*, a collection of stories and one-liners that have been sent to *The Globe* by Canadians from coast to coast.

I must warn you in advance that the humour in this book is not on a par with that of the *Royal Canadian Air Farce* or *This Hour Has 22 Minutes*. In fact, it's funnier. (Oops! That just slipped in.)

Seriously, it's the sort of corny stuff that Canadians laugh at while eating breakfast at a restaurant in New Glasgow, N.S., or in a donut shop in Red Deer, Alta., or at the kitchen table in Victoria, B.C.

It is not side-splitting or thigh-slapping hilarity. (I mean, can you imagine reading or hearing something so funny first thing in the morning that you laugh until your tummy hurts? You could have a heart attack! We certainly don't want *that* to happen!)

No, what follows are not jokes, but *smiles*. A Morning Smile is something that can make you feel good at the start of your day—something that you can tuck away and perhaps pass on to someone else a little later.

The nicest thing about it is that a smile doesn't cost much. As Dave Osborne of Coquitlam, B.C., wrote: "Smiles never go up in price, or down in value."

So there. Aren't you smiling already?

Norris McDonald
News Editor, The Globe and Mail

Acknowledgments

I would like to thank the following people: Grant Crosbie, General Manager, *The Globe and Mail*, for agreeing to finance this book; Michael Brophy, Vice-President, Human Resources, *The Globe and Mail*, for his advice and encouragement; Herbert R. Hilderley, President, ITP Nelson, for being so positive about the project; Colin MacKenzie, Managing Editor, *The Globe and Mail*, for suppressing his personal dislike of puns so that the exercise could take shape; William Thorsell, Editor-in-chief, *The Globe and Mail*, for chuckling out loud at many of them; Catherine Melville, my wife, for laughing out loud at all of them; *Globe* colleagues Anthony Jenkins, Brian Gable, Jane Christmas, Philip Jackman, and Geoffrey Rowan, for graciously agreeing to have their work reproduced in this book; John King, Deputy Managing Editor, *The Globe and Mail*, for helping me with the technical aspects of this work; Andrew Livingston, Tracy Bordian, and all the others at ITP Nelson for undertaking this project with such good nature; and last, but certainly not least, the hundreds of *Globe and Mail* readers—all Canadians—who cheerfully submitted Morning Smiles for publication. If they keep doing it, we'll just have to publish another book next year!

~1~

How It All Began

This was not a completely original idea. Over the years, people at The Globe—*notably Senior Editor J.A. (Sandy) McFarlane and Editor-in-chief William Thorsell—had suggested some form of reader participation for "Your Morning Smile." Nothing came of it, however, until Saturday, December 16, 1996, when I wrote the following column for page 2 of the paper.*

Smile, you could be on the front page

By Norris McDonald
News Editor

This was the Morning Smile that appeared on the front page of the paper a couple of weeks ago: "The Royal Family wishes the press would live by the motto Never say Di."

I read that joke and I laughed so hard that I just about busted a gut.

Hahahahahahahahahahaha!

Laugh? I thought I'd die.

All of *The Globe and Mail*'s Morning Smiles do that to me. I work really late at night. When I get home after midnight, my wife is usually asleep but she insists that I wake her up to tell her the joke that'll be on the front page of *The Globe* that day.

She doesn't want to have to wait until morning to read it.

So I sneak into our bedroom and I put my face down by her ear and I say: "Honeybuns, this one really cracked them up in the old composing room tonight. Here goes: 'Drama critics love the opening of the theatre season—it lets them stone the first cast.'"

First, my wife will start to stir. Then she'll start to giggle, and then to chuckle, and before you know it the bed is in danger of collapsing because she's bouncing up and down she's laughing so hard.

Hahahahahahahahahahahaha!

Apparently not everyone out there thinks the Morning Smile is as funny as my wife and I do.

In fact, there are people who actually think we should deep-six it, that there's no room for levity on the front page of Canada's National Newspaper. I found this out from Heather MacLeod, who is assistant to the editor-in-chief and the person who monitors *The Globe*'s reader-feedback line. This is what she had to say on the subject of the Morning Smile:

"I never took a call from a reader who said they liked it. Most people who comment on it think it's silly, that it's dumb. It's a pet peeve for some."

This would not be good news for the man who invented the Morning Smile, the late George McCullagh, who was publisher in 1936 when *The Globe* and *The Mail and Empire* merged to become *The Globe and Mail*.

According to Senator Richard Doyle, Editor-in-chief of the paper for many years, Mr. McCullagh felt strongly that there should be some amusement on the front page every day.

"*The Globe and Mail* was launched during the Depression, and there wasn't a lot to laugh about," Mr. Doyle recalled. "Mr. McCullagh wanted something in the paper that would accentuate the positive and that's how the Morning Smile came about.

"In the beginning, he tried several things, short jokes and such. For a while, he ran a small column written by Gracie Allen, but eventually he went back to the one gag on page 1."

Mr. Doyle said he was aware of Morning Smile criticism during his tenure at the paper. "But I learned a long time ago that those who don't like something will write, while those who like something won't write. Although some people wrote to complain, the vast majority didn't and I took this to mean they enjoyed it."

Mr. Doyle had one afterthought, before hanging up: "Now that I'm in politics, I can say this: There's a lot of crap in the paper these days that takes up much more space than the Morning Smile."

I thought this was such a great line that I had to repeat it to my wife in the middle of the night, and after she calmed down from her hysterics she said that I should put it in the paper, which I am now doing.

Most of the Morning Smile contributions come to us from the Los Angeles Times Syndicate. They are created (or purchased and edited) by a gag writer named Harlan Collins, whose main claim to fame is a pocketbook entitled *2,500 One-Liners For All Occasions*.

I know, I know. I can hear the harrumphs already. Canada's National Newspaper buys jokes from a U.S. company?

I'm not going to go into the reasons for this state of affairs, but if any of you Morning Smile critics out there think you can do better, I am inviting you to try to be funnier than Harlan Collins.

Send us a joke for the Morning Smile, and if our panel of judges—me—thinks it's good enough, we'll put it in the paper and give you the credit. Your name will be in type not much bigger than this, but what the heck—it'll be on the front page of *The Globe and Mail*.

My fax number is 416-585-5642. Give it a try; make me laugh, in 20 words or less.

The last time I can recall a challenge like this was in 1969, when a contest was held among *Globe* staff to come up with an original Morning Smile to appear on the front page of the first-moon-landing edition.

Copy editor Lois Scott was the winner. Her submission: "One astronaut to another: 'Look, there's Miami over the moon!'"

I read that and laughed so hard that I almost gave myself an attack of asthma.

Hahahahahahahahahahahaha!

~2~

Smiles

That column appeared in the Saturday newspaper. By Sunday, the first of the Smilefaxes had arrived and by Monday we were swamped. Here are some that made it into the newspaper, plus some that didn't.

If you want to get back on your feet after Christmas, just stop making your car payments.

Phyllis Taylor, Abbotsford, B.C.

Why don't bees celebrate Christmas?
Because they're humbugs!

Julian Sidebottom, age 10, Toronto, Ont.

The trouble with Christmas?
Not enough Ode to Joy; too much owed to everyone else.

David Godman, Scarborough, Ont.

Holiday photos—people on a roll.

Bob Aldis, Guelph, Ont.

Church choirs are reminded that Bach-Sing Day will be observed on Dec. 26, as usual.

Name withheld by request, Lethbridge, Alta.

Mrs. Claus has an essential role to play. She is one of Santa's subordinate clauses.

Bill Bolstad, Regina, Sask.

I don't care who you are, Fat Man, get those reindeer off my roof!

Ray Mack, Port of Belledune, N.B.

Social climber: Is it okay to eat chicken with your fingers? Etiquette expert: No, you must eat your fingers separately.

Esmond Choueke, Montreal, Que.

The male chauvinist refused to go to the hit musical because he thought it was called Les Ms.

Hugh Miller, North Vancouver, B.C.

A horse walks into a bar on New Year's Eve.
The bartender says, "Hey, why the long face?"

John Dawson, Sidney, B.C.

Worry about what you eat between New
Year's and Christmas, not the other way
around.

Vic Harradine, Kanata, Ont.

Leftovers: For a bird that doesn't fly much,
that turkey sure went a long way.

Don Flemming, Ottawa, Ont.

Why is six afraid of seven?
Because seven eight nine.

Elizabeth Hilson, age 6, Toronto, Ont.

What is it called when a surgeon removes the
decorations from a Christmas tree?
A tinselectomy.

Norman Rogers, Toronto, Ont.

TV documentary: The Making of Orange Juice
—a.k.a. Pulp Friction.

Paul C. Vincent, Winnipeg, Man.

Why do cows wear bells?
Because their horns don't work.

John Borden, Toronto, Ont.

Low-budget remake of The Silence of the Lambs: Ewes Be Quiet.

Christine Ford, Barrie, Ont.

What do Saskatchewan farmers do after the harvest?
They eat all they can, then can what they can't.

Brian Thrippleton, Oakville, Ont.

Sign in a poultry shop on Granville Island, Vancouver: Ask us about our Frequent Fryer program.

W.A. (Tony) Southwell, Victoria, B.C.

A termite walked into a bar and asked:
"Is the bar tender here?"

Connie Phillips, Scarborough, Ont., and S. Kelly, Waterloo, Ont.

A grasshopper walks into a bar. "Hey," says the bartender, "we have a drink named after you."
"Huh?" replies the grasshopper. "You have a drink named Nigel?"

Naheed Nendhi, Toronto, Ont., and Tarra Riley, Calgary, Alta.

Yasser Arafat won the election in Palestine by a sandslide.

Max Royer, Calgary, Alta.

Two horses meet on the street and one says to the other: "Gee, I remember your pace but I just can't place the mane."

Esmond Choueke,
Montreal, Que.

If a polar bear sits too long on an iceberg, does it get polarhoids?

George Leo Kraemer,
Kitchener, Ont.

Dyslexic agnostics with insomnia often stay up all night wondering if there's a dog.

James Kramer, Ottawa, Ont.

For vacations, may we suggest the British Virgin Islands, the U.S. Virgin Islands or the Italian Extra Virgin Islands.

Gillian Tsintziras, Toronto, Ont.

In Winnipeg, it's so cold they have to wear gloves to surf the net.

Barbra Duke, Winnipeg, Man.

Teacher's humour: "My jokes are so corny, I should be teaching in Nebraska."

Terry Burns, Dartmouth, N.S.

The Morning Smiles are getting so corny, it's absolutely amaizing.

Gordon W. Schmidt, Toronto, Ont.

Two psychics meet on the street. One says to the other, "You're fine, how am I?"

Cliff Hendler, Thornhill, Ont.

An African antelope walks into a bar. The bartender says, "Have I seen you before?" The antelope replies, "No, I'm gnu around here."

Tony Chandler, Sidney, B.C.

The best thing about landing on your head when skating is that you don't have to go far for ice.

Mike Bordynuik, St. Catharines, Ont.

Old age: when actions creak louder than words.

Bill Jones, age 81, Ajax, Ont.

The Russians have gone on-line—they're on the Internyet.

Martin Barker, Toronto, Ont.

One good turn gets most of the blankets.

Betty Bell, Mississauga, Ont.

For security reasons, Prime Minister Jean Chrétien is to receive police training, after which he'll be known as Jean d'arme.

Ken Ganczar, Winnipeg, Man.

Canada truly is a winter wonderland. Every winter, I wonder what I'm doing here.

Paul Carre, Toronto, Ont.

The length of a minute depends on which side of the bathroom door you're standing.

Sumeet Vadera, Markham, Ont.

Sibling warfare tactic: search and annoy mission.

Ann Mackay, Etobicoke, Ont.

How do they guard against crime at McDonald's?
They have a burger alarm.

Abshir Abdiladif, London, Ont.

What do you call the classification for poorly designed lamp posts?
A substandard standard standard.

Brent Cyca, Ottawa, Ont.

Poet's Corner: a high rhyme area.

Ken Burman, Willowdale, Ont.

An octopus goes into a bar and says, "Seven beers, please, and a glass of lemonade for the driver."

Tony Chandler, Sidney, B.C.

Good hecklers know the tricks of the tirade.

Howard Dellimore, North Vancouver, B.C.

After an hour in my doctor's waiting room, I now know why he calls his customers "patients."

Dave Duncan, Calgary, Alta.

How do you start a firefly race? Ready, set, glow.

Bonnie Haskin, age 8, Aurora, Ont.

Why did the elephant leave the circus? Because she was working for peanuts.

Emily Taylor Hall, age 4, Mississauga, Ont.

The name of the fixed link between New Brunswick and Prince Edward Island is rumoured to be Span of Green Cables.

Dan Chase and Tim Cross, Halifax, N.S.

Are opponents to the fixed link between New Brunswick and Prince Edward Island to be known as rebels without a causeway?

Peter Oldfield, North York, Ont.

Suspected Unabomber Ted Kaczynski's cabin didn't have indoor plumbing. Uncanny.

A.A. Peterson, Langford, B.C.

Ode to McDonald's, having worked on farms: E.I., E.I., WOE!

Anthony Miller, Tryon, PEI

The British are worried about the threat of rabies from European animals—the bite at the end of the Chunnel, perhaps?

David Braide, Toronto, Ont.

Why Canadian men don't take mistresses: Who wants two women telling you that you can't play hockey?

Sean Fine, Toronto, Ont.

If the Conservatives and the Reform Party unite, they could be called the Reformatories.

S. Nadkarni, Toronto, Ont.; Sonja Boyce, Edson, Alta.;
David Prieb; Toronto, Ont.; and John Cheesman,
Mississauga, Ont.

How about the Preservatives?

Paul Vincent, Winnipeg, Man.

~3~

More Smiles

We also started to receive Smiles via e-mail. In fact, there was an avalanche of Smiles from the Internet. Here are some of them.

Home for profit-sharing hens: the chicken co-op.

David Jansma, Toronto, Ont.

The difference between the Royal Canadian Air Farce and the Canadian Armed Forces is that only one of them is supposed to be a comedy troupe.

John Bailes, Toronto, Ont.

Greg Norman's collapse at the Masters: Drama on the high tees.

Gordon D'Cruze, Mississauga, Ont.

Instead of giving the politicians the keys to the city, it might be better to change the locks.

Connie Phillips, Scarborough, Ont.

How does a single woman get a cockroach out of her apartment? Ask for a commitment.

C. Chidley-Hill,
Toronto, Ont.

John Nunziata, John Nunziata, What an optimist is he! Thought the Grits would keep a promise, Thought they'd scrap the GST!

F.P. Hughes,
Hawkesbury, Ont.

A turtle was roughed up by some snails at the Oyster Bar. The investigating officer asked for the facts. The turtle said: "I don't know, everything happened so fast."

Rick Choma, Kingston, Ont.

New stores are opening in the Himalayas to sell medical supplies to mountain climbers. They're called Sherpa's Drug Mart.

David Barber, Toronto, Ont.

Why did the man get fired from the orange juice factory? He couldn't concentrate.

Marcus Leon, Toronto, Ont.

What did the chicken say when its mother
laid an orange?
Gee, look at the orange mama laid.

Jo Ann Conway, St. John's, Nfld.

Why do dogs sniff hydrants?
They're checking their P-mail.

Stephen Wells, Ottawa, Ont.

While working in the cornfield, a farmer used
a cellphone to call his spouse.
"Darling," he said, "I'll be late for lunch.
I can't find my way out of this maize."

M. Rohatynsky, Saskatoon, Sask.

Funny how an eight-hour workday can seem
like an eternity, yet eight hours of sleep is
over in the blink of an eye.

Peter Cronsberry, North York, Ont.

A fellow went into a coffee shop and the notice
on the cup said roll up the rim to win. So he
rolled up the rim and it said play again. So he
rolled it back down and rolled it back up and it
said play again. So he rolled it back down and ...

The staff of the Sheraton Halifax, Halifax, N.S.

Learn to plan ahead: it wasn't raining when
Noah built the ark.

Dave Osborn, Coquitlam, B.C.

I like the idea of pagans believing in more than one God. Come judgement day, if they don't like the verdict, they can ask for a second opinion.

Claudette Vandervelde, Campbell River, B.C.

Did you hear about the Buddhist monk who didn't want his mouth frozen when he had his teeth pulled? He wanted to transcend dental medication.

Jeff Morrison, Toronto, Ont.

What do seagulls use to write their letters? BirdPerfect.

Michael Kibbee, Toronto, Ont.

Never do today what you can put off till tomorrow or you will soon be out of a job.

Marshal Ney, Victoria, B.C.

Newfoundland and Labrador—children of a lesser cod.

Ted Kesik, Toronto, Ont.

The cry of migrating tundra swans arriving at their Canadian breeding grounds: "Take me to your Leda."

Vyvyan Bauer, Hensall, Ont.

If flashing green lights are advanced, are all the others beginners?

Corey Meingarten, Scarborough, Ont.

Whenever I pass by a church, I stop in for a visit. So when at last I'm carried in, the Lord won't say, "Who is it?"

Reg. S. Dougherty, Victoria, B.C.

One cannibal to another, while eating a clown: Does this taste funny to you?

Barry Gordon, Toronto, Ont.

Support group for people who talk too much: On-and-on Anon.

Graham Stillwell, Renforth, N.B.

If you had everything, where would you keep it?

Kate Brisland, Toronto, Ont.

McDonald's has a new burger for seniors— the Fallen Arch.

Jan Warren, Whitby, Ont.

Health club slogan: We leave no stern untoned.

Jennifer McIntyre, Toronto, Ont.

Did you hear about the new restaurant on the moon? Great food, but no atmosphere.

Israel Switzer, Toronto, Ont.

You can lead a horde to culture, but you can't make it think.

Zsolt Sizigetvari, Montreal, Que.

She called her dog Diamond because his first word was ruff.

F. Roly Hill, Saskatoon, Sask.

Not every fairy tale begins with "Once upon a time"; some begin with "After I am elected."

Bruce McAndrew, Kitchener, Ont.

If a cob of corn falls in a cornfield, does anybody ear?

Joe Pavia, Kitchener, Ont.

Europe: what the umpire says when it's your turn at bat.

Nick Cornish, Trenton, N.S.

Downsizing is not always bad. Remember that the ancestors of birds were dinosaurs.

Vic Kanbergs, Don Mills, Ont.

Teaser on literary magazine cover: What's Updike? Bugs Bunny Interviews America's Foremost Novelist.

Gideon Forman, Toronto, Ont.

France has the Riviera, sunshine and sand. The United States has Florida, sunshine and sand. Canada has Nun-av-ut.

E. Eberle, Toronto, Ont.

Where do shepherds vacation?
Bah Harbah, Maine.

Mike Jacka, Rothesay, N.B.

~4~

Long Smiles

Humour can take many forms. Most Morning Smiles are one-liners, two at most. But The Globe's *"Facts & Arguments" page periodically publishes humorous essays looking at the lighter side of the human condition. This one, by* Report on Business *reporter Geoffrey Rowan, caught just about everyone's eye.*

TVs in the bedroom: there is an up side

BY GEOFFREY ROWAN

I like to think that I'm a pretty open-minded guy, but for a while now my wife has wanted me to do something between the sheets that, well, that I just didn't want to do.

She wants to watch television in bed.

I knew when we were married eight years ago that she wanted to put a television in the bedroom, but she never really pushed too hard. I'd make up some statistic about bedroom TVs and sterility, quickly change the subject and that would be the end of it for a while.

But it would resurface from time to time, usually if one of us was home from work nursing a flu. Admittedly, daytime TV can be a great sickbed distraction, probably because it requires only semi-consciousness to appreciate.

"If we had a TV in the bedroom," she pointed out helpfully during my last bout of influenza, "you wouldn't have to camp out on the family-room couch."

A good point. The bathroom is a flight of stairs away from the family room but just a few steps from the master bedroom.

"You'd be able to snooze, watch Regis and Kathy Lee, snooze, throw up, snooze, watch Oprah, and you never have to climb the stairs or lie there while the kids act out *Hop On Pop* on your aching head," she said.

It was a seductive argument, especially to someone being squeezed by a stomach virus; especially to someone whose feverish sleep was being interrupted regularly by the playing of Barney tapes so worn from use that the painfully familiar songs and dialogue sounded like they were being delivered underwater.

But the fever eventually broke, the food eventually stayed down, even the warbly musical stylings of the purple dinosaur became bearable, or at least escapable, and the TV-in-the-bedroom discussion faded into the background.

In recent months, however, my wife has been raising the subject more often, and now with two kids, the sterility gambit doesn't impress her much.

She came back from a business trip, recalling how pleasant it was to open her eyes in the morning, in a strange hotel bed, and see friendly, familiar faces— *Canada A.M.*

And how helpful it was to get caught up on the news of the day while running around getting dressed.

But if we had a TV in our bedroom, I countered lamely, there'd be nothing special about going away on business.

Then we bought a new bed, which was such a vast improvement over the misshapen thing that had predated our relationship that any excuse to spend more time there seemed a good idea. I began to waver.

After referendum night I was tottering. Dinner had been eaten, kids bathed, booked and bedded, the dog walked, and still the results trickled in. Rarely have I felt so much like pulling the covers over my head.

But I clung stubbornly to my position, so stubbornly in fact that I had to wonder at my intransigence and finally, examine it. I found that, like most positions unthinkingly held, it was born of fear.

This is tough to admit because few people at *The Globe and Mail* will even acknowledge owning a television set, and when they do it's usually because they picked one up at a flea market, intending to make it into an art deco aquarium for their exotic fish, or put it to some other charmingly eccentric use.

Not me. I have watched *The Simpsons* and I have laughed.

Still, I feared getting too close to TV, letting it work its insidious way too deeply into my life. Putting one in the bedroom might be the first step down a slippery slope toward a complete loss of self.

I would quit reading in bed, I wouldn't play with the children, or get them fed and dressed in the morning, or get myself fed or dressed in the morning.

My wife is, of course, substantially less nuts.

She is of the self-possessed school of thought that prescribes hard work, enjoyable leisure and generally getting through life with as little unnecessary muss and fuss as possible.

Seeing the fundamental weakness of my logic, she decided to put me away on this matter once and for all.

A TV in the bedroom is just a TV in the bedroom, she said. It's not a metaphor for our intellectual and moral decay or a precursor to the decline of the family and Western civilization. Sometimes a cigar is just a cigar.

"Besides," she said in her most playful I-know-something-you-don't-know voice. "If we had a TV in the bedroom, we'd spend more time in bed together, and what could that hurt?"

I called the cable company the next day.

Have you ever wondered why some drivers appear to be worse than others? Maybe it's because they can't see—or admit that they can't see. Philip Jackman, a reporter and editor at The Globe, *drew chuckles with this contribution.*

Hey! Who moved the sidewalk?
(Or how I got my first pair of glasses)

BY PHILIP JACKMAN

It has come as something of a shock, having these strange, glass-filled objects perched in front of my eyes. When you're 47 and have never worn spectacles in your life, adjusting to such cumbersome visual aids takes some doing.

Not that I really need them, you understand. They're just a mild prescription to sharpen things up a bit. My long-distance vision was getting just a little blurry, that's all. I'm convinced my wife was exaggerating when she said I couldn't read street signs until we were so close it was impossible to make a turn without rolling the car. And the small matter of me missing the sign on Highway 400 that said "BARRIE— 4 INTERCHANGES" was just a minor misunderstanding.

Anyway, I went to the ophthalmologist to get my eyes checked. Not that I really needed to, you understand.

The ophthalmologist put drops in my eyes to dilate the pupils and made me read rows of letters on charts that were very blurry at the bottom.

Obviously a cheap printing job. Next, she asked me to read some passages from a card up close, which I did with consummate ease. She then had me look through various lenses. Finally, the diagnosis. "You have astigmatism," she said, "and myopia. That's why you can still read up close at your age."

What did she mean, "astigmatism"? What did she mean, "myopia"? What did she mean, "at your age"? Then came the coup de grace. "I'm giving you a prescription for trifocals."

I reeled. I had walked in there with perfectly good eyesight and suddenly I was being told I was triply visually challenged. And wasn't astigmatism something to do with bleeding from the palms on religious holidays? My thoughts were still racing when I stepped from her office and the bright morning sunshine hit my dilated pupils, causing me to cry out in pain and clutch my hands to my eyes. As I staggered to the car I realized I knew how Count Dracula feels when Vincent Price flips the lid off his coffin on a sparkling July afternoon.

The next step in the spectacle saga was the visit to the optician. He explained that with trifocals, the top part of the lens is for long-distance viewing, the middle part for middle distance and the bottom part for reading. For an extra charge I could have specially ground lenses that didn't show the joins. I opted for these. Wearing glasses was going to be bad enough without staring through streetcar tracks.

I picked up the glasses a few days later. It was a revelation. As I stepped into the street, I discovered that I was no longer six feet tall, but had been reduced to somewhere around 3 foot 6. The ground was only a yard below my chin. This made stepping on and off the sidewalk highly perilous. An escalator became an object of terror.

However, I persevered. My first major outing with specs was to shop at Ikea. Have you noticed how much they've improved that store recently? Everything's so clear and bright and, well, visible. For instance, you can now read product signs such as Sklarvort, Sokka and Slag from hundreds of feet away. I was also impressed at how all the products are within easy reach of someone only 3 feet 6 inches tall. They really have done a wonderful job.

The following day I was out driving, and to my huge surprise I discovered that, despite Ontario's massive cutbacks in public-sector spending, the highway signs had all been replaced with larger, clearer ones. And that signpost on Highway 11 for the mysterious town of ORDUNEG had been corrected to read ORO LINE 6. However, I did notice that, no matter how many times I hit the lever to wash the windshield, a bunch of annoying specks refused to disappear.

And then there was the first day at work wearing my new sight enhancers. While some colleagues did notice that I was suddenly sporting specs, others stared at me quizzically and asked if I had had a haircut.

Or lost weight. Some enquired whether I had a new pair of glasses.

Meanwhile, I have discovered that there are some peripheral advantages to wearing eyeglasses. One is that it opens up a whole new topic of conversation with fellow wearers. You can compare prices, discuss the relative merits of myriad frames and lenses, trade stories of pulling your sweater off over your head and losing the things for several hours. It's a subject almost as inexhaustible as computers or golf.

Then, of course, glasses make great props. You can stare over the top of them to express disapproval. You can take them off, place them wearily on the desk and pinch the bridge of your nose to imply massive tedium at being asked a thoroughly stupid question. But where they really score is when it comes to what I call diversionary cogitating.

Suppose you're in a meeting, the boss has asked you a question and you don't have the faintest idea what the answer is. You remove your glasses.

You dangle them by one of the earpieces while staring thoughtfully at the ceiling. You suck on the end of the earpiece and appear to be on the brink of uttering a Great Truth. You carefully replace your specs, look thoughtfully at your questioner and change the subject. Your colleagues have been so hypnotized by this display that no one notices.

In light of such advantages, I suppose I'll come to accept wearing glasses. I'll just look at them as one more milestone on life's highway, that road leading ultimately to decline, death and, we hope, an afterlife devoid of asymmetrical federalism.

So I guess I'll keep them. Not that I really need them, you understand.

In medieval times, knights would go off to the joust, leaving their wives at home to do the washing and to complain. Then men invented golf. Then cyberspace arrived on the scene. Globe editor Jane Christmas struck a nerve with many women when she wrote the following.

Internet widow: A tale for our times

By Jane Christmas

His mornings used to start so peacefully. Up at dawn, he'd throw on some clothes, head downstairs, make his coffee and saunter outside to commune with nature beside his pond.

The slam of the screen door was my cue to wake up. Passing the bedroom window, I would see him at the opposite end of our yard sprawled in his worn Muskoka chair gazing into space, clenching his mug of java.

Like telepathy, we instinctively knew what the other was doing and by the time I had trundled downstairs to the kitchen, he was coming in the back door to refill his mug and say good morning.

Our evenings were just as bucolic: After the children were in bed, we'd pour a glass of wine, catch a bit of TV or engage in a game of Scrabble.

This had been our routine for years, until one morning this spring when I passed the bedroom window and did not see him taking in the morning air. In a panic I ran downstairs and found him hunched over in the family room, his face illuminated by a soft glow. My worst fears were confirmed: My nature boy was in a heat-lock hypnosis with Ms. Internet.

That my husband had traded me in for computerized intelligence was shocking enough. But that he tried to draw me into a kind of ménage à trois was downright shameful. The morning I first caught him with Ms. Internet, he barely lifted his gaze from her fluorescent eyes: "Guess what, I'm in Harvard's library right now! Wanna see?" I politely declined. Watching someone show off their computer gymnastics is about as interesting as watching home movies.

That night, as we stumbled through the door after a long day at work, I instinctively reached for the wine glasses. His instinctive role has been to bring out a bottle of vino, but tonight he grabbed the laptop instead and turned on the TV. Welcome to the '90s version of the cold shoulder, I thought.

Still I persevered, thinking a glass of wine and a neck rub would thaw him out. Wrong. As I walked into the room he barely acknowledged me, although his excitement was boundless: "Guess what? I've found this really neat site that shows the planets rotating. Wanna see?" Clearly, he was in a universe of his own. My brain had logged off for the day but Ms. Internet's was at full throttle. I picked up a book and went to bed.

At 2:30 a.m. I awoke to discover my husband wasn't beside me. I found him exactly where I had left him $4^1/_2$ hours earlier. "Guess what? I'm in the White House! Wanna see?" I turned around and stomped back upstairs.

Our life's been like that ever since. Although he doesn't golf, I am beginning to understand the plight of the golf widow. In a way, being an Internet widow is worse: He's there but he's not. At least if he were golfing he'd be physically out of the house and I could turn my angst toward something productive—like cleaning out the closets. Instead, extension cords litter almost every room in our house and serve as a constant, painful reminder of his philandering. (You have no idea how tempting it is to want to accidentally trip over one of these when he and Ms. Internet are having a tête-à-tête.)

My husband will insist he's not spending a lot of time on-line, but I know his interest in me has diminished. Our intimate moments are non-existent. About the only thing that's up these days is the lid to his laptop.

It's not that I haven't tried to recapture his attention. Armed with the ultimate weapon in any self-respecting woman's arsenal—the Victoria's Secret catalogue—I have amassed a small wardrobe that would attract the attention of Heidi Fleiss. Unfortunately, it hasn't had the desired effect on my husband. Unless that bustier's packing a modem, I doubt he'd be able to tell it apart from a T-shirt that reads "I'm with Stupid."

I figured the relationship with the Byte Babe would have waned by now. Maybe his eyeballs would fall out, or, at the very least, his eyesight would diminish significantly. There was a glimmer of hope last month. A bucket of cold water appeared in the form of the phone bill. There, in black and white, was evidence that he was two-timing Ms. Internet with Ms. E-mail. Our monthly $60 phone bill had ballooned to $250. He sheepishly admitted his addiction and promised to curb his habit.

It will take a while to clear this hurdle in our marriage, to get our lives back on track. The garden is overgrown with weeds, the paint on the house is peeling, and there's a long list tacked to the fridge of small but necessary home repairs to attend to. But right now, my husband and Ms. 'Net are still involved in that early stage of steamy passion where they just can't get enough of each other. When they're curled up on the sofa together, she takes him to places he's never been; he follows along willingly, unable to resist the temptation of foreign sites.

I figure World Wide Web jet lag will eventually sideline him. As for her—I hope she gets a virus.

~5~

Even More Smiles

For every Smile we publish, there are about a dozen that we don't. It's not that we don't like them; we just don't have room for more than one a day. Here's a salad of some that went in and some that didn't.

Everything is pretty basic...
Until you have to do it yourself.

Jaan L. Luubert, Unionville, Ont.

What did Sir Isaac Newton think when the apple fell on his head? "Glad it wasn't a brick."

Eric Adams, Toronto, Ont.

Firefighter's motto: put the wet stuff on the red stuff.

Garry Parker, Winnipeg, Man.

Daydreamer's motto: A little reality goes a long way.

H.G. McCaslin, Regina, Sask.

Newfie who turned out a bad batch with his home-made still found he had an impediment in his screech.

Frank Young, East York, Ont.

What did Lady Macbeth say to her dog?
Out, out damned Spot.

S. Macre, Toronto, Ont.

Most lawyers believe Jesus Christ must have been a lawyer as he, too, could walk on water.

Jozef B. Glowacki, Toronto, Ont.

When a woman is ready to throw in the towel, she launders it first.

Mrs. R. Sack, Willowdale, Ont.

The pet rabbits we purchased were not "one of each gender." "Missy" was actually "Mister." Now he is "Miss it."

Rolf Eliason, Guelph, Ont.

Remembering Mom's advice to wear light-coloured clothing outdoors at night, I did—and was run over by a snowplow!

Ruth Smith, Toronto, Ont.

It is impossible to be in two places at once, except if you live on the border.

Andrew Moore,
Downsview, Ont.

Slogan on a frog's tee-shirt: Time's fun when you're having flies.

Shawn and
Nick Robins,
Victoria, B.C.

A man died after a car repeatedly honked at him. Police said it was a drive-by tooting.

Charles Crockford, Waterloo, Ont.

Our tax dollars at work? Government researchers have proved that sex is hereditary. If you and your wife never have it, your children won't.

Dale Charbot, Kingston, Ont.

The problem with most half-baked ideas is that they're not thawed out ahead of time.

Stephen Babey, Calgary, Alta.

Sign on a pet-grooming store in Victoria: "The Barking Lot."

Bill Bolstad, Regina, Sask.

I like to relax in a bathtub with a good book. One day, I'll try it with water in it.

Ritchie Miyashita, Toronto, Ont.

 The weaker sex is really the stronger sex because of the weakness of the stronger sex for the weaker sex.

Lois Grant, Calgary, Alta.

The only difference between onions and bagpipes is that nobody cries when you cut up the bagpipes.

Don Dafoe, Sarnia, Ont.

At least in Hell, no one will say, "Have a nice day."

Marni de Pencier, Toronto, Ont.

Life insurance is when you bet the insurance company that you're going to die someday and the company says, "Oh no you're not ..."

Cal Orok, Toronto, Ont.

Trait of channel surfer who can watch a
program for more than a minute:
Remote Pause Ability.

Eric Harrison, Burlington, Ont.

The older a man gets, the further he had to
walk to school as a boy.

Kevin Milburn, Toronto, Ont.

Betting on the horses is like plastic surgery—
you pays your money and you picks your
nose.

Heinz Wiggeshoff, Toronto, Ont.

The new corporate vision for Environment
Canada's weather service and weather
channel? Compressed Air.

Ian Burton, Toronto, Ont.

News item: Several cows were killed when a
cattle truck overturned. Names of the victims
are being withheld pending notification of
next of kine.

Art Stone, Windsor, Ont.

"Why are you divorcing at ages ninety-seven
and ninety-two?" "We wanted to wait until
all the kids were dead."

Kurt Rothschild, Toronto, Ont.

Definition of an elected politician:
the oaf of office.

Glenn Cochrane, Toronto, Ont.

Film about a cranky, intellectually challenged
man who rose above his circumstances:
Forrest Grump.

N.L. Greenaway, Oakville, Ont.

Marriage can be like a bath. After a while, it's
not so hot.

R. Templeton, Toronto, Ont.

The prostitute-cum-hockey player's first
penalty? Two minutes for hooking.

Cliff Luis, Toronto, Ont.

Man does not live by bread alone; he needs
circuses too.

Nick Evasiuk, Athabasca, Alta.

Anyone who enjoys gambling can go to Hull.

Ralph Atkinson, Toronto, Ont.

News item: "Rare owl eaten in African
village." Who gives a hoot! Anyone the wiser?

Edward W. Barrett, Montreal, Que.

The dog star dazzles the late winter sky—
Siriusly!

Gillian M. Hancock, Hull, Que.

Percautionist: a drummer who practices safe
sex.

Peter Mosher, Toronto, Ont.

Egotist's favourite song: I Got Me Babe.

Bruce McCain, Milton, Ont.

Scientists have discovered global warming.
Who, then, can explain why it's getting colder
and colder?

D. T. A. Michels, Toronto, Ont.

I called up the wrestling association. They put
me on hold.

Martin Barker, Toronto, Ont.

I have nothing but vowels, said the Scrabble
player disconsonantly.

André Blom, Waterloo, Ont.

The hockey player-turned-comedian couldn't
get away from using his schtick.

Santino Petrucci, Mississauga, Ont.

Those who blow their own horn deafen others.

Ina Currie, Lindsay, Ont.

A musical instrument played by a pair of sheep: Tuba!

Judy Cole, Owen Sound, Ont.

In my day, the politicians were fat and the budgets were skinny.

Paul Carre, Toronto, Ont.

Who's at your doorstep every morning? Your "Globe Trotter."

Susan Rayner, Toronto, Ont.

Two wrongs do not make a right—but 3 lefts do.

Greg Chaban, Georgetown, Ont.

What do you call someone who doesn't like to use E-mail? An E-mail chauvinist.

Wayne Paulson, Ottawa, Ont.

Whoever said, "Go with the flow" never heard of waterfalls.

Suzy Marcinkow, Sarnia, Ont.

On urban poop-and-scoop laws: it's a turdy job ... but someone has to do it!

Bart Guthrie, Toronto, Ont.

How to become a successful con man: Fake it.

Philip Stenning, Toronto, Ont.

Recent sign observed at book publishers' convention: MISSPELLERS OF THE WORLD—UNTIE.

Robert Mitchell, Weston, Ont.

Never play poker with American west coast fishermen—they're too good at filling an inside straight!

Richard Walpole, Victoria, B.C.

Said one sheep to the other: "We've got to stop bleating like this."

Parker T., Toronto, Ont.

Bob Dole—banana republican.

Naveed Alam, Kingston, Ont.

You know what the problem with a lot of people is? Overpopulation.

Larry Kuntz, Toronto, Ont.

Why can't a bicycle stand up on its own?
Because it's two tired.

Tony Chandler, Sidney, B.C.

Name for a funeral parlour: Remains to be
Seen.

Joseph Torbay, Cambridge, Ont.

Why do they call them oncologists if they're
rarely on call?

Eric Mendelsohn, Toronto, Ont.

The poet called it poetry, the critic called it
unjustified prose.

Tucker Carrington, Richmond Hill, Ont.

Mechanized farming will always have its
detractors.

Simon Farrow, North Vancouver, B.C.

If male deer have antlers, do female deer
have unclers?

Thomas Curran, Gloucester, Ont.

Why do fluorescent lights hum when you
turn them on? Because they don't know the
words.

Rick Preston, Ajax, Ont.

From the middle of a group of youngsters rough-housing in a playground, a voice rang out: "Stop that, or I'll give you a half-Chrétien!"

Peter Woolstencroft,
Waterloo, Ont.

A doctor we know has a yacht named "Healing Time."

N. Bingham, Victoria, B.C.

Life's a beach—but sometimes it gets washed away.

Michael Jordon, Kingston, Ont.

Have you ever noticed that the people who should have inferiority complexes never do?

Nancy Douglas, Etobicoke, Ont.

What do you call a fly with no wings? A walk.

Neil Maclean, Halifax, N.S.

There are three kinds of people in the world—those who can count and those who cannot count.

Ken Ganczar, Winnipeg, Man.

How does a grizzly build his home?
With his bear hands!

Kimberlee Regan, age 8, Leaside, Ont.

Information, like water, has to be filtered
before it is fit to consume.

Doug Campbell, Niagara Falls, Ont.

Said the priest to the man who cheated his
parish on some church repair work:
"Repaint and thin no more."

Ben Chambers, New Westminster, B.C.

Life is too short for 1-ply tissue.

Terry Franklin, Scarborough, Ont.

A quarter horse is so named because it has
two bits in its mouth.

Arnie Lind, Regina, Sask.

A way for Steven Spielberg to capitalize on
the movie-going public's fascination with
huge dinosaurs and cute pigs: Jurassic Pork.

Peter Strachan, Pickering, Ont.

Bumper sticker: "Lead me not into
temptation ... I can find it myself."

John H. Leonard, North Vancouver, B.C.

~6~

Different Smiles

Some people insist on phoning in their Morning Smile contributions. This can result in newsroom levity, as the reporter or editor who takes the call then relates the Smile to his or her colleagues. Interruption of serious work follows. At these times the Editor is not amused.

The technophile and the technophobe
aren't as different as once thought.
The phobe has crashed a hard drive
while the phile, to date, has not.

Ron Charach, Toronto, Ont.

Spring and summer: That time of year when
rain showers provide water for the lawndry.

Sonja Boyce, Edson, Alta.

The ban on unpasteurized cheese: Just one
more federal attack on Quebec culture.

Dennis Kolba, Halifax, N.S.

Those new sunglasses for babies: A shade
pretentious.

Gideon Forman, Toronto, Ont.

The Candlemaker's Prophecy: There will be
no wick for the rested.

Bob Long, Toronto, Ont.

Four-year-old Winnipegger upon arrival in
Vancouver during Spring Break, "Mommy,
how come they have green snow and we have
white snow?"

Lisa Ruta, Winnipeg, Man.

When two rap music groups compete, the
score always reads forte forte.

Stewart Brown, Peterborough, Ont.

Person on the phone to a friend about to go
on a motor-tour of England: "Be sure to drive
on the right side of the road!"

Vladimir J. Pimenoff, Willowdale, Ont.

The Doctor's Dilemma: capitation or
decapitation?

Walter R. Stewart, St. Mary's, Ont.

Rain—well-connected showers.

Dave Osborne, Etobicoke, Ont.

We no longer have hummingbirds at our window feeder. Someone showed them a songbook ... with all the words.

Doug and Barbara Wood, Charlottetown, PEI

Native leader Ovide Mercredi, excluded from the private talks at the First Ministers Conference, attempts to gain admission by telling RCMP security, "It's okay I'm with the band."

Harvey Silverstone, Toronto, Ont.

What do you call someone who keeps saying, "Gimme, gimme"?
A Gimme-Pig!

Emma Kelesay, age 5, Toronto, Ont.

What part of the cake are hockey players most familiar with? The icing.

Yoni Mernuk, age 8, Toronto, Ont.

How did Chicago win the NBA finals?
They were remarkabull.

Yoni Mernuk, Toronto, Ont.

Was the lengthy article on penile enlargement politically erect?

Bert Raphael, Toronto, Ont.

Where birds go to unwind: Crowbar.

Jeffrey S. Morry, Winnipeg, Man.

Item: Toronto Maple Leafs hike ticket prices for the 1996–97 season.

Bob Sheppard, Oakville, Ont.

The Dutch Elvis Impersonator's most requested song: "Blue Spruce Shoes."

Kevin Casselman, Kingston, Ont.

Guess if you turned an upstairs bedroom fan upside down and drilled holes in the ceiling, you'd be called a fanatic.

John A. Miles, Scarborough, Ont.

Overheard on the ocean bed: "Dear, cod we tonight? Just for the halibut? Not now, I have a haddock."

Doug B. Yam and J.S. Yormark, North York, Ont.

Young boy: Magician, what is the most dangerous trick you know?
Magician: When I was 12, I learned to saw people in half.
Young boy: Magician, do you come from a large family?
Magician: I have many half-brothers and sisters at home!

Jo Ann Conway, St. John's, Nfld.

Where early 20th-century art is concerned, I do not care for the Surrealist ... my heart belongs to Dada.

Martin Boyaner, Montreal, Que.

There is an infinite amount of toothpaste in a tube. You just have to squeeze really, really hard.

Brent Cyca, Ottawa, Ont.

"Everyone is doing it! Get on side!" shouted the lemming.

*F.P. Hughes,
Hawkesbury, Ont.*

DING
A
LING.

What does the singer Meatloaf call his servants? Hamburger helpers!

*Bob Gruhl,
St. Catharines, Ont.*

It's no fun to loaf around if you don't have the bread to do it.

Joyce Irving, Kitchener, Ont.

When asked to comment on the proposed offshore rig, the oil executive said, "It augers well for the future."

David Godman, Scarborough, Ont.

You peel the outside, you cook the inside. You eat the outside and throw away the inside. What am I? Corn on the cob.

Lori Goldberg, Don Mills, Ont.

Escaped prisoner: I'm free! I'm free!
Kindergarten kid: Big deal, I'm four.

Jessica Bulgutch, North York, Ont.

University: An institution where the professors take over the job of lecturing your kids.

Darrell Cheung, Waterloo, Ont.

Why do astronauts feel they are the butt of jokes? People are always sending them up.

Randal Marlin, Ottawa, Ont.

Vegetarians eat vegetables. Beware of humanitarians.

Fenella Smith, Stouffville, Ont.

We hear the farmers of Canada are forming a union. They're calling it the E.I.E.I.O.

Stewart K. Henry, Dalhousie, N.B.

In today's business world, if you're not paranoid, you're just not paying attention.

John Hamilton, Waterloo, Ont.

Constitutional
nightmare for hunters:
The right to arm bears.

Michael Derblich,
Toronto, Ont.

What did the butcher
do with his
inheritance? He went
on a chopping spree.

Don Miles,
Salt Spring Island, B.C.

A war is being waged against Malaria. What
have those Malarians done now?

Patrick Unan, North York, Ont.

What's Canada's most popular antiperspirant?
Unemployment insurance.

Tony Deveau, Calgary, Alta.

Did you hear about the two peanuts in the
park? One was a salted.

Rick Preston, Ajax, Ont., and Sid Smith,
Niagara-on-the-Lake, Ont.

Sign in bank window: If you have money to
burn, let it smolder here.

Don Zacher, Willowdale, Ont.

Young Johnny came home from Sunday School somewhat confused after the morning lesson. He asked his dad, "What does it mean, Thou shalt not commit agriculture?" After some thought, his father replied, "Son, that just means you're not supposed to plow the other man's field."

Peter D. Hambly, Hanover, Ont.

If you keep an air-freshener in your office, you'll have something in your working life that always makes scents.

Jim Wyse, St. John's, Nfld.

What is the difference between Scarborough and yogurt? Yogurt has culture.

Donald Rossiter, East York, Ont.

Where does the king keep his armies? In his sleevies!

Jennifer Hesing, Halifax, N.S.

Procrastination: A big word that takes a l-o-n-g t-i-m-e t-o s-a-y.

Stuart Hickox, Toronto, Ont.

If it's true that money talks, all it ever says to me is "Goodbye!"

Chris Neal, Ottawa, Ont.

Cannibal personnel manager's favourite part of the job: Staff turnover.

P. Dance, Orillia, Ont.

Sign outside a photo studio:
Someday your prints will come.

R.A. Sinclair, North Bay, Ont.

Do you know why tires are sold with no air in them? Because of the inflation!

Michel Grenier, Montreal, Que.

Many a round figure has been acquired by eating too many square meals.

Rasheed Mohamed, Toronto, Ont.

Mixture of apples, oranges, bananas, pineapples and small colourful parrots:
Fruit cockatiel.

Tim Scapillato, Wakefield, Que.

How can you turn a negative into a positive?
Simple, short-circuit it!

Louis Gagnon, Kingston, Ont.

"This is Revenue Canada. We've got what it takes to take what you've got!"

Cheryl M. Ryshpan, Thornhill, Ont.

What did the circus manager say when
Dextro the human cannonball passed away?
"Where will we find another man of his
caliber?"

Michael Dentante, Toronto, Ont.

One solution to the problem of short-term
memory loss is to wait a while.

Tony Oostenbrink, Edmonton, Alta.

A penny saved is a penny taxed!

Don Beaupre, Deep River, Ont.

A man with a beer belly has his best years in
front of him.

David Townson, Milton, Ont.

The puppy limped into town on crutches with
a pistol around his waist and declared:
"I'm looking for the guy who shot my paw!"

Esmond Choueke, Montreal, Que.

Printed on a jogger's T-shirt:
"I have a WAIST to go."

Jay Courtland, Toronto, Ont.

Financial crisis: When there's not enough
month at the end of the money.

Jack Bryson, Montreal, Que.

Man at post office: "100 years ago the mail went by horse. It took 5 days to get a letter across the country. Now it takes 10 days. Why?" Postal clerk: "Those poor horses are a lot older now."

J. Bryan Whealen, Toronto, Ont.

They met in a revolving door and they've been going around together ever since.

M.J. Alward, Toronto, Ont.

The gardener who doesn't know which peat moss to use has no sense of humus.

Rosanne Steinbach, Toronto, Ont.

There is very little future in being right— when the boss is wrong.

Marilyn Rickard, Toronto, Ont.

Did you hear about the guy with an ego problem—he went looking for an "I" doctor.

Jim Rose, Edmonton, Alta.

~7~

Smiling People

Canada has its share of semi-professional humorists—people who are often well-known in their own communities, but not elsewhere. We are indeed fortunate to hear from some of them often.

PAT McALPINE

"Your Morning Smile" has a number of regular contributors: Charles Crockford of Waterloo, Eric Mendelsohn of Toronto, Bill Bolstad of Regina, the Mernick family of North York, Hugh Arscott of Saskatoon, and so on. The list could continue just about forever.

Naturally, we can only use occasional submissions from these folks, as the competition for Morning Smile space is fierce. We also have to be democratic with "Your Morning Smile," and ensure that as much of a geographic distribution is maintained as possible. (What this means is that the joke might not be so hot but if it's from Nova Scotia and we haven't had a submission from Nova Scotia for a while, it'll see print before we use another one from Toronto. Get it?)

The heavyweight champion of these "regulars," however, is a jokester named Pat McAlpine, a high school teacher from

Nepean, Ont., who can be found most days cracking up the students at St. Paul's High School. Mr. McAlpine is married with three daughters and is known around his neighbourhood as the Punmeister of Bell's Corners.

When he faxes something down to *The Globe and Mail*, he doesn't submit just one potential Smile, he sends fifty!

"I'm such an opunionated fellow, I should be sentenced to a stretch in Kingston Punitentiary," he said the first time we talked.

He might be right. He starts every day in his classroom with a joke. At home, he puts up a Joke of The Day on the lamppost in front of his house. His neighbours complain if he goes away for a weekend and the joke stays the same for two or three days.

Only once has one backfired.

"When the Ontario Minister of Community and Social Services was having a hard time early in his tenure, I wrote a bunch of welfare jokes and mailed them off to my local MPP. On the back of the envelope, I wrote 'Opun Carefully.' The staff in his office saw that and called the police and they came and took away the letter and blew it up. That's the only time I've ever bombed."

Mr. McAlpine's motto? A smile is a carnation in the buttonhole of life.

Here is a sampling of his humour.

Graduation Goodies

The perfect graduation gift for an 18-year-old girl used to be a compact. Still is—but now it has four wheels.

It's amazing how many students had trouble being punctual during their high school years. They must have graduated "Summa Cum Later."

Graduation time is when a mother says to her daughter, "Of course daddy remembers his grad dance. That's why he wants you home at the stroke of midnight."

Graduation—a time when grads go in for some serious reading: the want ads.

Holiday Cheer

At Christmas we can make people forget the past with a present.

'Twas the night before Christmas,
and all through the house,
not a creature was stirring
—no spoons!

A kid came home from the Christmas concert at school and the parents asked which Christmas carols they'd sung and the kid said, "Oh, the one about the king that no one liked." "We don't know that one," said the parents. "Oh yes, you do," replied the kid. "It's the one about King Wences, the louse."

Who sings "Love Me Tender" and makes Christmas toys? Santa's little Elvis.

Santa finishes delivering his presents just in the St. Nick of time.

In December, we sing "Jingle Bells." In January, we sing "Juggle Bills."

As Vincent Van Gogh's plastic surgeon said to him on December 31: "Happy New Ear!"

Easter is the time of year when it's okay to put all your eggs in one basket.

Life in General

Did you know that Alexander Graham Bell invented the telephone on Mother's Day? His mother said she'd kill him if he didn't call.

I laugh up my sleeve, because that's where my funny bone is.

Laughter will add years to our lives and life to our years.

The sundial is an old-timer.

If we take up the law, we're lawyers. If we lay down the law, we're parents.

The Ottawa Lynx wear stockings with a lot of runs in them.

Teacher: Give me a sentence with the word "unaware" in it.
Student: When I get up each day, I put on my unaware.

Cook's favourite song—"The Bastings in Life Are Free."

A hockey player's favourite holiday—St. Hat Trick's Day.

The Zamboni driver's favourite song—"I Only Have Ice for You."

One good thing about cooking outdoors: it keeps the flies out of the house.

HUGH ARSCOTT

Mr. Arscott is a life insurance underwriter—among other things—in Saskatoon. He's been writing one-liners for years and sending them to his local paper, *The Star-Phoenix*. They sometimes print them. Every autumn, he publishes a booklet of his best gags and other observations on life and sells it as a Christmas stocking stuffer. He turns the profits over to the Salvation Army. His Morning Smile contribution at the time of the Quebec Referendum was a classic:

Bouchard's Motto—If at first you don't secede, try, try again.

Here are a couple of others, courtesy of Mr. Arscott.

Lucien Bouchard wanted to be the premier of Quebec in the worst way and he's proving that every day.

The reason there is only one female egg and tens of millions of male sperm is because men will not ask directions.

Sure, farmers are fervently praying for good harvest weather but so are merchants, car dealers, and bankers. Only travel agents and ski-hill operators pray for an early winter.

Real hockey fans can follow the puck on the radio.

FROM OTHER (FREQUENT) CONTRIBUTORS

What did the rooster say when it was
umpire? "Balk, balk, balk."

Moshe Mernick, age 10, Downsview, Ont.

Patient: I ate a bone.
Doctor: Are you choking?
Patient: No, I'm serious.

Yoni Mernick, age 8, Downsview, Ont.

What do Elizabeth Taylor and Jean Chrétien
have in common? Separation anxiety.

Garrett Wasny, Vancouver, B.C.

Notice outside church:
Despite the huge deficit, the wages of sin
remain absolutely the same.

Rt-Rev. G. Russell Hatton, London, Ont.

Why did the Canadian cross the road?
To get to the middle.

Joseph Trainor, Toronto, Ont.

Remember, if you are not the lead dog, the
view never changes.

Russ Wallace, Halifax, N.S.

Which side of the chicken has the most feathers? The outside!

Samantha Mein, age 6, Nepean, Ont.

A pessimist is a well-informed optimist.

Alain Goupil, Sherbrooke, Que.

Definition of an optimist—a civil servant who brings his lunch to work.

Patricia Parsons, Gander, Nfld.

Now that the Blue Jays have signed Cito and Joe, what's next? A line of Gord Ash jeans?

Ken Trew, Barrie, Ont.

At a mass execution during the French Revolution, the guillotine operator said, "Necks, please."

D. Black, Toronto, Ont.

Facing a firing squad, the three men were asked about their last wishes. The first, a minister, said: "I wish to deliver a sermon that would stir my congregation like never before." The second, a cantor, said: "I wish to sing the 23rd Psalm with such feeling that it would reach the gates of Heaven." The third, a layman, said: "I'd like to be the first one executed."

Chaim Weinberg, Downsview, Ont.

A guy called his doctor and said every time he put on his hat he heard music. The doctor removed the band.

Randy Burnett, North Bay, Ont.

What did the lawyer wear at the aerobics workout? A class action suit.

Helmuth Schumann, Toronto, Ont.

As the universe unfolds, one likes to think that God has a Plan B.

Robert Marjoribanks, Ottawa, Ont.

It looks like Canada's military troubles are finally coming to a Boyle.

John Bull, Willowdale, Ont.

And then there was the ornithologist at the airline check-in counter declaring his crow carrion luggage.

Jack Corr, Ottawa, Ont.

Did you hear about the newborn who refused to breast-feed? He much preferred womb service.

Tim Donais, Ottawa, Ont.

Child philosopher: Play-doh.

Erene Augustine, Toronto, Ont.

The mad scientist developed a universal solvent but couldn't find anything to keep it in.

Ross Rogers, Muskoka, Ont.

Who's the funniest boxer of all time?
Willie De Witt.

H.G. McCaslin, Regina, Sask.

Did you hear about the guy who refused to work with Microsoft products? He didn't do Windows!

D. Brevner, Richmond, B.C.

Summer clothes: summer paid for, summer not.

Nick Cornish, Trenton, N.S.

New business in casino city of Orillia, Ont.— Bed and Broke fast.

M. Rupke, Woodbridge, Ont.

Then there was the English Literature professor who finished his unit on William Shakespeare and started his unit on Ben Jonson: he went from Bard to verse.

J.F. McGuinness, Surrey, B.C.

Dole sees his running mate Kemp on an airplane and says, "Hi, Jack." Pandemonium.

Lataranee Punjabi, St. John's, Nfld.

For all that Dole spent on his campaign, all
he got was a quarter back.

Alex Eisen, Toronto, Ont.

Although the Democrats may feature a
photograph of the young Clinton shaking
hands with President Kennedy, the
Republicans are suppressing the photo of the
young Dole shaking hands with President
McKinley.

Eric Mendelsohn, Toronto, Ont.

Lucky are we
who watch TV,
For we're never without
a Dole Moment.

David M. Bishop, Toronto, Ont.

People get into financial difficulty because they
buy things they don't need with money they
don't have to impress people they don't like.

Frank Stefanik, Vancouver, B.C.

If a farmer wants his hens to increase their
output, does he egg them on?

Edward Baxter, Stratford, Ont.

Let a smile be your umbrella, if you don't
mind getting your teeth wet.

John A. Boone, Kingston, Ont.

What did the beekeeper say when asked if he was going to buy bees from Bangkok? "Thai bee or not Thai bee, that is the question."

Charles Crockford, Waterloo, Ont.

What did the butcher say to his girlfriend? We can't go on meating like this.

Frank Thirkettle, Calgary, Alta.

Why was the amoeba prison so small? It had only one cell.

Gustave Yaki, Calgary, Alta.

Is it true that in Australia women police officers are known as Sheila cops?

Frank Stephen, Scarborough, Ont.

The 'WHITHER?' Channel

~8~

Ear-to-Ear Smiles

Parents sometimes send in Morning Smiles and attribute them to their children. Or else, jokes that have them rolling on the ground of the schoolyard are transmitted verbatim. Either way, sometimes they make it and other times they don't. Here are a few examples, along with more of the adult variety.

What do you call a person with books in their pockets? Smarty pants.

> *Ray Suhanic-Hazlitt, age 4$\frac{1}{2}$, Islington, Ont.*

Why did the dragon cross the road?
Because there were no more chickens.

> *Anna Limeback, age 4$\frac{1}{2}$, East York, Ont.*

Fashion designers and economists have much in common. Both do the most with the least material available.

> *Bob Jeffries, Aurora, Ont.*

A man falls asleep on the psychiatrist's couch. The psychiatrist mumbles: "Well, we can rule out stress."

Bill Bolstad, Regina, Sask.

Caesarian Section: the best seats in the Amphitheatre.

Donald J. Cameron, Pembroke, Ont.

Definition of a professional: Someone who can remain bored in the face of excitement.

David Lasker, Toronto, Ont.

A last request before the guillotine: I'd rather have a bottle in front of me than a frontal lobotomy.

Santino Petrucci, Mississauga, Ont.

Luck is the inadvertent application of great skill and superior knowledge.

Walter G. Prevaling, Winnipeg, Man.

If it takes two pints to fill a quart, how long will it take to Philadelphia?

Austin Morris, Peterborough, Ont.

The damsel whose car has a flat battery would be in need of a white knight to gallop up on a charger.

Tony Chandler, Sidney, B.C.

Minor surgery is defined as surgery that someone else has.

John M. Stoffman, London, Ont.

Perrin Beatty magic act: Now you CBC, now you don't.

Kelly Connelly, Halifax, N.S.

One of the nice things about being a great singer is that you have those large resonating chambers where your brains ought to be.

Anna Russell, Waterloo, Ont.

In medieval times, fearing bad breath, the defenders of the castle took "Battle Mints."

Martin Boyaner, Montreal, Que.

How about the cat that ate some cheese, then waited by the mouse hole with "baited" breath?

John Dawson, Sidney, B.C.

Did you hear about the shampoo tycoon? He left everything to his heir.

Jason Brooks, Ottawa, Ont.

What happened to the gal who waited too long for her ship to come in? Her pier collapsed.

Roger Reeves, London, Ont.

The scientist claimed to have crossed a frog and a toad. It turned out to be a frod.

Jack McIver, Toronto, Ont.

It may be fatal to rig a mortise for a dead bolt.

P.A. Hallam, Don Mills, Ont.

You know that you are getting older when your favourite section of *The Globe and Mail* is "From the Archives—25 years ago."

Ed Murphy, Ottawa, Ont.

Marriages should be like mortgages. Closed and renegotiable every five years or fully open for years with no penalty attached.

Steve Rakus, Toronto, Ont.

What do you get when you cross a sad French Canadian singer with an Italian dessert? Tears of Mitsou.

Eric Goddard, Toronto, Ont.

Junius refused to play the Blue Danube Waltz in march time because that would be submitting to an arbitrary measure.

Eric Mendelsohn,
Toronto, Ont.

No man is an island, yet every baby is incontinent.

Larry Rossignol, Toronto, Ont.

Recent Hollywood film whose title answers the question, "Which bird calls shall I make?" Just Cause.

Tom St. Louis, Toronto, Ont.

How do you put the spark back into your relationship? Start by walking across a shag rug.

Elizabeth Goldsmith, Ottawa, Ont.

If a judge took a photograph of himself delivering a verdict, would that be a snap decision?

Charles Crockford, Waterloo, Ont.

You know you're having a bad day when your voice mail has laryngitis.

Londos D'Arrigo, Toronto, Ont.

So Canada is sending peacekeepers to Haiti.
Onward Chrétien soldiers.

Bert Raphael, Toronto, Ont.

The difference between a fiddle and a violin is
a tuxedo.

Ed Murphy, Ottawa, Ont.

When he finally got it all together, he forgot
where he put it.

Gordon Greene, Waterloo, Ont.

If you do your best, whatever happens will be
for the best.

Vir Kashyap, Toronto, Ont.

Where there's a will, there's an inheritance
tax.

Sam Swaminathan, Toronto, Ont.

Beware of geeks bearing disks.

John A. Ferguson, Toronto, Ont.

Medical term: Svelte is the vay your ankles
get ven dey are sprained.

Randy Burnett, North Bay, Ont.

Top bureaucrat: Lord of the files.

Jerry Edenson, Toronto, Ont.

I tried to write a letter to Lucien Bouchard,
but I couldn't think of anything to say. I
guess it was a case of writer's Bloc.

Tim Scapillato, Ottawa, Ont.

How come the kids on the catalogue covers
keep their clothes so clean?

F.P. Hughes, Hawkesbury, Ont.

Capitalist junk mail: Modern American
literature.

Heather Hodgon, Regina, Sask.

Those who do not find time for exercise will
have to find time for illness.

Keith Kostek, Edmonton, Alta.

Snake addressing a crowd: "Ahem, ka-hum—
Excuse me, I seem to have a frog in my
throat."

Chris Allen, Halifax, N.S.

What do you call the balding men in a ski-lift
lineup? A receding chair line!

Tom Kenworthy, Calgary, Alta.

Independence Day: Four explosions and a
wedding.

Colleen Doucet, London, Ont.

A vacuum cleaner—the only thing you buy that you hope sucks!

Elaine Rotor, Ottawa, Ont.

What do you call a lawyer with an IQ of 50? Your honour.

George Dunbar, Scarborough, Ont.

How many English Canadians does it take to name the national holiday? Two: One to call it Canada Day and the other to call it Dominion Day.

Jim Mason, Richmond Hill, Ont.

What do Americans call July 4? The Fourth of July.

Jim Mason, Richmond Hill, Ont.

One woman to another, at a birthday lunch: "So, how old are you?" Reply: "I just turned 27—U.S."

Brenda Adams, Ottawa, Ont.

Have you seen Prince Charles' wardrobe lately? He's dressing for succession.

Kenneth Downey, Mississauga, Ont.

Spitball: A saliva slider.

D.T. Bath, Peterborough, Ont.

If one synchronized swimmer drowns, do the rest have to drown too?

Joseph Kicak, Toronto, Ont.

If we work too hard, we get stressed out. But after a relaxing holiday, we never get stressed in.

Ben Griffin, Burnaby, B.C.

Old grammarians never die. They just come to a full stop.

Karl Dore, Fredericton, N.B.

The optimist believes Earth is the best place there is. The pessimist fears this is true.

Sarah Jones, Toronto, Ont.

Do overwrought farmers suffer from "barn out?"

M.A. Kavanagh, Calgary, Alta.

If you want to be remembered forever, all you have to do is forget to send a thank-you note for a wedding gift.

Nancy Bishop, Islington, Ont.

After-school programs at the Olympic Stadium: Extra Funicular Activities.

Frank Manley, Montreal, Que.

If the Chinese alphabet has more than 5000 characters, how big is their can of Alphaghetti?

Terry Whitehead, Lethbridge, Alta.

Practice safe sex: use condoms.
Practice safe government: use kingdoms.
Practice safe English: use conundrums.

Bill Sturrock, Sidney, B.C.

Did you hear about the man who refused to eat sausages for breakfast? He said that would be going from bed to wurst.

Michael Thomas, Gananoque, Ont.

If a chicken coop had four doors, would it be a chicken sedan?

Adam Slim, North Vancouver, B.C.

God has trouble with *Hymn Sing*. She doesn't know who it's directed to.

Ray St. Arnaud, Victoria, B.C.

Last Christmas, we bought our Dad a Shopvac. He says it's just sitting in the basement, collecting dust.

Peter Stokes, Kingston, Ont.

Did you hear about the cook who wanted to double the recipe but the oven wouldn't go to 700 degrees?

Jay Nathwani, Toronto, Ont.

Why didn't the dinosaur cross the road? Because it hadn't evolved into a chicken!

Tom Sommerville, Toronto, Ont.

If I order a pizza-sized direct-to-home satellite dish and it isn't delivered within 30 minutes, do I get it for free?

Brant Scott, Ottawa, Ont.

What one strawberry said to another: See what a jam you got me in!

Bert Armstrong, Owen Sound, Ont.

What did the priest say to his vegetable garden before delivering his sermon? Lettuce pray.

Fred Davis, North York, Ont.

You know how you go out and buy a newspaper every morning? So does Conrad Black.

Douglas Ng, Toronto, Ont.

Ottawa watering hole for Quebec separatists: Bar-BQ.

John Feld, Toronto, Ont.

If marriage is a mystery, then to be married to two people at the same time is a bigamystery.

Mel Whitney, Penticton, B.C.

Rule of thumb for evaluating computer technology: If it works, it's obsolete.

Mike Kohut, Yellowknife, NWT

A man with a phobia for German sausage always fears the wurst.

Mike Epplett, Kingston, Ont.

Time flies like an arrow, fruit flies like a banana.

Dustin Troy, Toronto, Ont.

Two men walked into a bar. You would think the second one would have seen it.

Katherine Angus, age 8, Toronto, Ont.

Knowledge is a funny thing. It's hard to pick up, but easy to carry.

Sam Frizell, Oakville, Ont.

Why is it that Canada Post delivers the mail, while in England, the Royal Mail delivers the post?

David Segal, North York, Ont.

Love is waking someone up at 3 a.m. for a diaper change.

C.J. Orok, Gravenhurst, Ont.

Two silk worms in a race ended up in a tie.

Ken Taplin, Langley, B.C.

Sex therapist: A pubic relations expert.

Elvino Sauro, Toronto, Ont.

Does the ban on sex imposed by Swimming Canada include the breast stroke?

Lippe De Haan, Exeter, Ont.

~9~

Never-Ending Smiles

Earlier this year, the family of Dr. Walter Wingate Nichol submitted a contribution from their Dad and asked that we publish it on his birthday. We couldn't, but did get it into the paper about a month later. Dr. Nichol's Smile—the World's Shortest Poem—started what we like to call "Competition Smiles," where readers see a Smile one day and try to better it the next. We always get a flood of entries when something that's seen as a "Competition Smile" appears. Here are samples.

World's Shortest Poem:
Mink'll wrinkle.

> *Dr. Walter Wingate Nichol,*
> *Mississauga, Ont.*

World's Shortest Poem II:
Fleas—Adam had 'em.

> *Ogden Nash (with thanks to Ted Kemp, Sarnia, Ont.; Sheila Wright, Ottawa, Ont.; Luis Fernandes, Toronto, Ont.; D. Patrick Ryan, Calgary, Alta.; Fred Kerner, Willowdale, Ont.; Jacques Lafortune, Montreal, Que.; Barb Malcolm, Saint John, N.B.; and James Gordon, Hornby Island, B.C.)*

World's Shortest Poem III: I, why?

Edward Ozog, North York, Ont.; Carro Braunlich, Willowdale, Ont.; and John Stewardson, Toronto, Ont.

Tired? Fired.

Jay Booker, Vancouver, B.C.

Orville Wright: I fly.

Fred Kerner, Willowdale, Ont.

Sid hid.

Jon R. MacNeill, Saskatoon, Sask.

O, no.

William Shakespeare
(Juliet, upon finding Romeo dead)

Hope? Nope.

Allon Beck, Calgary, Alta.

Drinker's lament: Why rye?

Charles Crockford, Waterloo, Ont.

World's shortest love poem:
Charles, tu dors?
Non.
Alors.

L.M. Sebert, Ottawa, Ont.

Absolutely the world's shortest poem:
T.
V.

John Snell, Toronto, Ont.

Absurd.
In a word.

L. Johnson, Holland Landing, Ont.

DESCARTES

Mark Leahy of Ottawa sent us this Smile about French philosopher René Descartes.

I am, therefore I think. That's putting
Descartes before the horse.

Look what followed.

Descartes walks into a bar. The bartender
says, "Would you like a beer?" Descartes says,
"I think not." Descartes disappears.

Naheed Nenshi, Toronto, Ont.; Tarra Riley,
Calgary, Alta.; and David Braide, Toronto, Ont.

Descartes described how his father taught
him to swim by throwing him into the Seine:
"I sink, therefore I swam."

Peter deNiverville, Moncton, N.B.

As a student, Descartes couldn't afford a
room with water, so he bathed in the Seine.
"I stink, therefore I swam."

Max Leggett, Toronto, Ont.

The student who attended a funeral rather
than philosophy class was said to have put
the hearse before Descartes.

Lili Rachnitzer, London, Ont.

Descartes, explaining his love of theatre:
"I act, therefore I ham."

Ed Kortes, Victoria, B.C.

Descartes, explaining why he left the party after flirting with the wife of a jealous man: "I wink, therefore I scram."

Peter deNiverville, Moncton, N.B.

Descartes, responding to the toast on Robbie Burns Day: "Aye drink, therefore a dram."

Tom Carter, Edmonton, Alta.

RHODES SCHOLARS

This was another subject that drew dozens of responses. It's one of those Smiles, however, that can go on forever. We've cut them down to get as many in as possible.

If Ontario Transportation Minister Al Palladini succeeds in ridding Ontario of potholes, he could be called a Roads Scholar.

Keith Wigzell, St. Catharines, Ont.

If Al Palladini can be called a Roads Scholar, then surely Silken Laumann is more than worthy of being called a Rhodes Sculler.

David M. Bishop, Toronto, Ont.

If Al Palladini is a Roads Scholar, then Silken Laumann must be a Rowed Scholar.

Thom Mitchell, St. Catharines, Ont.

If Al Palladini is a Roads Scholar, and Silken Laumann is a Rhodes Sculler, perhaps Alfred Sung should design a Rhodes Collar.

Charles Crockford, Waterloo, Ont.

If Alfred Sung designs Rhodes Collars, they should be worn by traffic reporters who would be Roads Callers.

Christina Lewis, North York, Ont.

If Al Palladini is a Roads Scholar, and Silken Laumann is a Rhodes Sculler and Alfred Sung designs Rhodes Collars, the infant crying in the back seat is surely a Roads Bawler.

Bill McAndrew, Kitchener, Ont.

If Alfred Sung designs the Rhodes Collar, then Benetton should pick the Rhodes colour.

Claude Laurin, Gatineau, Que.,
and John Wipf, Regina, Sask.

It's time Tim Horton's invented a Rhodes Cruller.

> Jack Cobb, Montreal, Que.; P. Perehinczuk,
> Toronto, Ont.; and R. Van Steenes, Toronto, Ont.

The Globe's editors should be looking for a Roads Culler.

> Peter Thompson, Oakville, Ont.

If *The Globe* intends to keep this Rhodes Scholar joke going much longer, we'll all soon require Rhodes sigh assistance.

> Joe Phillips, Oakville, Ont.

Joe Phillips of Oakville grumbles that we'll all soon need Rhodes sigh assistance if *The Globe* keeps the gag running much longer. Might we say that Mr. Phillips is verging on Rhodes choler?

> Ian Weir, Langley, B.C., and Kay Brant,
> Agincourt, Ont.

It would appear that we are nearing a Cross Roads.

> Bruce Anderson, Nepean, Ont.

Pessimists are in need of Rhodes Scholard Glasses.

> Heather Young, Winnipeg, Man.

All Rhodes are paved with good pundits.

Raymond Levick, Willowdale, Ont.

If we took this joke show on the road, we'd need Rhodies.

Peggy Basle, Torbay, Nfld., and John F. Campbell, Toronto, Ont.

Ontario is at a cross-Rhodes.

Bruce Anderson, Nepean, Ont.

Could the Rhodes jokes please hit the Rhode?

Sam Frizel, Oakville, Ont.

Please turn those jokes into Rhodes kill.

Paul Chislett, Ottawa, Ont.; Mark Kubisz, Willowdale, Ont.; Cerith H.K. Wong, St. John's, Nfld.; and Jan Warren, Whitby, Ont.

Many roads are paved with stones, but *The Globe* Rhodes make me stumble in the morning.

Edith Rothschild, Toronto, Ont.

Smilefax punsters wear me down—they should all be called E-Rhodes Scrawlers.

Raymond Peringer, Toronto, Ont.

When all these jokes are over, let's all give a
big Rhodes holler.

P. Eprile, Toronto, Ont.

Any more Rhodes jokes and we may well
roam.

Peter Fraser, London, Ont.

If I telephone you one last Rhodes joke, will
you promise that I will be the last Rhodes
caller?

Bill MacIntosh, Dundas, Ont.

Did you know that bleach erodes colour?

Brendan Sullivan, Islington, Ont.

A plea to the editor after last week's Rhodes
kill pun-ishment: please, at least for a few
days, could you leave no groan unspurned?

D. Moles, Oshawa, Ont.

The pun's over when all Rhodes lead to
groan.

Graeme Taylor, no place provided

Enough already!

Bibi Tewarie, Toronto, Ont.

MAD COWS

Pity the poor cattle of Britain—and the poor British farmer. Their predicament was the subject of mirth around the world.

If the U.K. slaughters its cows, the country will be barren of beef.

Bryan King, Vancouver, B.C.

British farmer: "I just shot my cow."
Second British farmer: "Was she mad?"
First farmer: "She wasn't too happy about it."

George R. Chandler,
Castleton, Ont.

If the crisis in the British beef industry proves to be blown out of proportion, will history refer to it as Much Amoo About Nothing?

Bob Jones, Toronto, Ont.

If all the cows in Britain are destroyed because of mad cow disease, will it be known as "the herd that was shot 'round the world?"

Harold I. Schiff, Toronto, Ont., and
George Gerhardt, Victoria, B.C.

Survey on British food: Fish and chips?
Excellent. Roast beef? Offal.

John Cameron, Guelph, Ont.

Mad Cow Disease: Farmageddon.

Simon Farrow, North Vancouver, B.C.

With mad cow disease, the future of the U.K.
beef industry is at steak.

Oussama Mohtar, Ottawa, Ont.

First cow: "Are you worried about this mad
cow disease?"
Second cow: "Not at all, I'm a duck."

Tom Brownrigg, Guelph, Ont.

It took a Hogg to cry foul and beef up
Britain's cattle industry.

George R. Chandler, Toronto, Ont.

The single-masted, lateen-rigged boat sailed
an erratic course across the Red Sea. Another
case of Mad Dhow disease.

Chris Hicks, West Hill, Ont.

Must the magnificent Beefeater Guards at the
Tower of London now change their name to
the Madhatter Guards?

Lili Rechnitzer, London, Ont.

New sitcom about newlyweds running a cattle operation in Britain—"Mad About Moo."

Michael Osborne, Halifax, N.S.

British Mad Tory Disease—Thatcherosa Monetarium—a retro virus causing deficit attention disorder.

Eric Mendelsohn, Toronto, Ont.

TWOONIES

The new $2 coin brought a big response. Grin and bear it.

The new $2 coin coming out on Monday will have a picture of the Queen with a bear behind.

J.G. Keogh, St. Catharines, Ont.

If the new $2 coin has the Queen on one side with a bear behind shouldn't we call it a moonie?

Graham Finlayson, North Vancouver, B.C.

The new $2 coin should be called Lucien— because it wants to separate.

Owen and Leslie Saffrey, Scarborough, Ont.

What do the new $2 coin and a politician have in common? They both make the quarters in your hand look like nickels.

David Brown, Brantford, Ont.

So why not call the new $2 coin an American dollar?

Hugh Arscott, Saskatoon, Sask.

Let's spell it "twonie" because in Canada not even change stays the same.

Neale Ginsburg, Toronto, Ont.

If the new $2 coin wants to break in two, let's call it the "Quebuck."

Ian Grant, Victoria, B.C.

The new $2 coin is nothing more than a plugged nickel.

Ashoke Deb, St. John's, Nfld.

Given the rate at which the new $2 coins will depart our pockets, they should be called "too-da-loonies."

Ben Kranc, Toronto, Ont.

They should have put a pair of male deer on the back of the new $2 coin—then we could call it two bucks.

Rod Junor, Sudbury, Ont.

It should not be surprising that the twoonie is not well-liked. After all, people always resist change.

Doug Cliff, Victoria, B.C.

Daniel Black, 9, suggests the new $2 coin be called a twinkie because you always get two in a package and sometimes they are stuck together.

Bill Black, Mississauga, Ont.

PUNNIES

The response to the first Smile below was incredible. Unfortunately, we couldn't have used most of them, even if we'd had room!

Too bad about the poor baker who was electrocuted when he stepped on a bun and a currant went up his leg.

Paul W.J. Mingay, Markham, Ont.

Did you hear about the butcher who backed into his saw? He got a little behind in his orders.

Ian Johnson, Halifax, N.S.

Then there was the sparrow that flew into a fan and came out shredded tweet.

Ian L. MacQueen,
Saint John, N.B.

What about the launderer who backed into an iron and was depressed? Or the ewe that backed into a barbed-wire fence? She smiled sheepishly.

Bob Taylor, East York, Ont.

Unlike the butcher who got behind in his orders, a firefly who backed into an electric fan was delighted.

Sandy McFarlane, North York, Ont.

The optician who backed into his lens machine? Made a spectacle of himself.

Neill McRae, Victoria, B.C.; David Crossley, Saskatoon,
Sask.; and Glenys Gotham, Oshawa, Ont.

The bee who flew into the lawnmower? A belittling experience.

Lee Parpart, Kingston, Ont.

The racetrack announcer who backed into a lawnmower? They're off!

Paul Dion, Penetanguishene, Ont.

The dog that backed into a fan? Detailed.

Glen Tolhurst, Brampton, Ont.

MORE PUNNIES

And then we received an avalanche of submissions all patterned along the lines of this one:

What about the stewardess who backed into a propeller: disaster.

Thanks to Mariel Desjardins, Vancouver, B.C.; A.H. Heywood, Willowdale, Ont.; D. Rodwell Austin, Toronto, Ont.; John F. Campbell, Toronto, Ont.; Dominick Amato, North York, Ont.; Joseph Cook, Mississauga, Ont.; Jay Booker, Vancouver, B.C.; Tom deLayen, Toronto, Ont.; Don Cliff, Burlington, Ont.; J. Sheinin, Toronto, Ont.; Mel Goldberg, Ottawa, Ont.; John Stockwell, Peterborough, Ont.; John Figg, London, Ont.; Christopher Barrett, Kingston, Ont.; Douglas Sylvester, Ottawa, Ont.; Sean Brosnan, St. John's, Nfld.; Jeff Morrison, Toronto, Ont.; and Neil Smith, Markham, Ont.

There once was a pussycat, driven by fear,
Backed into a fan and was hit in the rear.
The results were most horrid,
The screaming was torrid,
It was nothing less than disaster.

David M. Bishop, Toronto, Ont.

The transvestite priest? Defrocked.

Dick Crosby, Toronto, Ont.

A politican who backs into a fan may be unseated but could return to work after a rebuttal.

Raymond Levick, Willowdale, Ont.

Is there no end to these jokes?

Ross Rogers, Muskoka, Ont.

LIFE ON MARS

We always have to be wary of what I like to call the Irritation Factor. If someone finds something funny, you can bet there's someone else who doesn't like it at all. We have to make sure some of these Competition Smiles don't go on too long. Here's an example.

Life has been discovered on Mars. Now they're looking for Reader's Digest.

Paul Wright, Comox, B.C.

If scientists have found Life on Mars, and are now looking for Reader's Digest, where do they find the Time?

Charles Crockford, Waterloo, Ont.

We'll just have to make Time. Either late Saturday Night or next Newsweek.

Cleo Mowers, Coaldale, Alta.

So they've found Life on Mars, are looking for Reader's Digest, but have no Time. Do you think they'll see any People? Or be hit by a Rolling Stone?

Ann Housepian, Montreal, Que., and
Karyn Kirk, Longueuil, Que.

With all those jokes about Life on Mars, it sure must have been a slow Newsweek.

Tony French, Wards Island, Ont.

Since the editors have given a lot of Time this slow Newsweek to let their Readers Digest the possibility of Life on Mars, they now should circle The Globe and Mail interviews to the Sun and Stars on Saturday Night.

David Daly, Calgary, Alta.

I hope that while they are looking in the Milky Way, they don't hear any Snickers.

Arthur Goldwasser, Willowdale, Ont.

Life on Mars? Slow Newsweek? Frankly, my dear, I don't give a damn.

Michael Jordan, Kingston, Ont.

Life on Mars? Someday, they might take a picture of our Globe and Mail it to us.

J.G. Montpetit, Montreal, Que.

For the real answer to the question of life on Mars, check out a Mars bar.

Thomas H. Gillman, Winnipeg, Man.

If you want to know what all the talk about life on Mars is about, try asking a Scientific American.

Peter Friedrichsen, Toronto, Ont.

Although jokes about Mars are in Vogue, isn't it driving you Mad? Let's be Frank, we need more Variety in our Life. Here's the latest: our Private Eye tells us it's Martha Stewart Living on Mars.

Deborah Danniels, Toronto, Ont,

Life on Mars? How many more elements will we be adding to the periodicals table?

Alan Nesmith, Whitby, Ont.

This week's contributors to Your Morning Smile are, apparently, in Vogue.

George Dunbar, Scarborough, Ont.

An Express Telegraph, delivered in Record Time by Saturday Evening Post, warns that this whole thing will Herald the rebirth of the Daily Planet. Could Mercury be next?

Stephen Cryne, Kitchener, Ont.

Now that we've established there's life on Mars, why don't we see if there's any intelligent life on Earth?

Tony Hirons, Toronto, Ont.

OLD DEANS

Here's another example of something that can get the Irritation Factor kicking into high gear.

Then there's the Old University Deans Society—they never die, they just lose their faculties.

Alvan Gamble, Ottawa, Ont.

Old university deans might lose their faculties, but old sculptors lose their marbles.

Charles Crockford, Waterloo, Ont.

Old lawyers lose their appeal.

Scott Van Alstine, Kelowna, B.C.

Old accountants become unbalanced.

Roland Prodaniuk, Edmonton, Alta.

Old engineers lose their designations.

Sidney Joseph, Thornhill, Ont.

Old teachers lose their principles and old doctors lose their patience.

Judy Yormark, North York, Ont.

Old geologists get petrified.

Bill Bolstad, Regina, Sask.

Old wrestlers and mountaineers both lose their grip.

Bob Taylor, East York, Ont.

DIFFERENCE LIMERICKS

And then there are the old-chestnut "Difference Limericks." Delightful and very original.

What's the difference between an optometrist and a fund raiser? One checks people's eyes and the other eyes people's cheques.

Rob Donelson, Waterloo, Ont.

The difference between a jail guard and a jeweller? One watches cells and the other sells watches.

Ann-Margaret Hovsepian, Montreal, Que.

A teacher and a train driver? The teacher trains the mind, and the driver minds the train.

Ijaz Qamar, Mississauga, Ont.

An out-of-work sailor and a blind horse? One can't go to sea and the other can't see to go.

George Dunbar, Scarborough, Ont.

Any more of these dumb jokes and we will cancel our subscription.

Anonymous